Outdoor Explorers
Planting and Growing

By Sandy Green   Photography by Chris Fairclough

Contents

FRANKLIN WATTS
LONDON•SYDNEY

Plants are all around

Trees, grasses and flowers are all plants. Have a look at what grows near you.

Visit woods, parks and gardens. Look at the trees, grasses, flowers and water plants.

Take some photographs to
record what you find.

- How much light and shade
is there in each area?
- How damp or dry is the
ground?
- Use what you see to help
you compare the needs of
different plants.

Print the photos and
group them into water plants
and meadow, garden and park plants.

Water plants

Meadow, garden and park plants

What's in the squares?

Mark out a one metre square on the ground using sticks. Repeat on a meadow, by a pond or stream and under some trees.

Look at what is in each square.

Use a magnifying glass to observe closely what you find.

On a square sheet of paper draw all the plants and minibeasts in each marked out square.

Look at your squares again the next day. What things were the same? Which were different? Talk about what you have found out.

Where were most changes found? Why was this do you think?

Glossary: **Observe** – to look carefully at something.

Let's explore seeds

Most plants grow from seeds. Think about where seeds come from, how different they can be and how they reach a place to grow.

Throw sycamore seeds into the air and watch them twirl round as they fall.

Sycamore seed

Blow dandelion seeds and watch them float away.

Make a picture using glue and lots of seeds from fruit and vegetables. What shapes have you found? How do they feel?

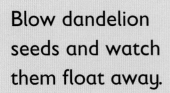
Here is the picture I made.

Get ready for planting

It's fun to grow plants from bulbs or seeds.

- Fill a pot with soil or plant compost.
- Dig a hole and put in your bulbs, one at a time.
- Cover the bulbs with soil or compost and press it down firmly. Water well.

Glossary: **Compost** – rotted down plants.

- To grow plants from seed, scatter the seeds very carefully where you want them to grow.

- Sprinkle soil or compost over the top of them and water them well, too.

Bulbs and seeds all need water to grow properly.

Make a composter

Compost helps plants grow strong and it is easy to make.

Compost is made from vegetable and fruit peelings mixed with dead flower heads and roots.

It looks like soil when it is ready to use.

- Collect uncooked scraps and garden waste.

- Fill a large sweet jar with the scraps and garden waste.

- Put on the lid.

- Get an adult to punch holes in the lid to let in air.

- Leave the jar in a corner of the garden.

How long does it take to turn to compost?

Collect and press flowers

Flowers make lovely pictures but they die and go brown very quickly. Pressed and dried flowers last much longer.

Collect a few flowers from places where there are plenty of the same type. Small garden flowers press well. Never pick flowers without asking permission.

Glossary:
Permission – being told it is ok to do something.

Wing nut

- Use a flower press if you have one. Put the flowers between sheets of kitchen paper.

- Screw the wing nuts very tight.

- After a few weeks the flowers dry out and will be ready to use.

If you don't have a flower press, cover your flowers with kitchen paper and stiff card and put heavy books on top of everything.

We made lovely pictures with our flowers.

Trees

Leaves

Branches

Trunk

Roots grow underground

When you plant a tree seed, it takes a long time to grow tall. Every tree will eventually have roots, a trunk and branches of leaves.

A very young tree is called a sapling. Plant some saplings in your garden at home or at school.

Beech and mountain ash saplings are easy to grow.

We planted a mountain ash sapling.

Conkers are the seeds of the horse-chestnut tree

I planted a horse-chestnut sapling.

Trees with the biggest trunks are usually the oldest. Some trees can live for hundreds of years.

What trees can you find in your area? How big are they? Can you reach all the way round them with your arms?

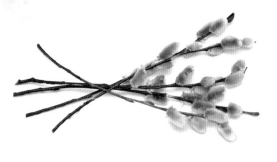

Watch roots grow

Find a pussy willow tree.

Pussy willow buds

This isn't the right tree!

• Cut a few branches from the pussy willow tree. Remember to ask permission first and ask an adult to help you.

• Place the branches in a glass jug. Half fill with water.

• Keep topping up with water and watch the branches put out roots. This will happen over the next two to three weeks.

Explore pond plants

Visit a pond or stream. How many different plants can you see.

Be careful around water and make sure an adult is nearby.

Water lilies float on the surface of the water. Frogs, toads and newts like to sit on them.

Tall reedy plants grow close to the water's edge. This is a good place to watch dragonflies and damselflies flitting about.

Plants help keep pond water healthy. Without plants some fish and pond creatures will die.

Glossary:
Collage – a picture made from small pieces of paper and material.

A miniature garden

Make your own miniature garden using an old seed tray filled with a thin layer of soil.

Find things to use from all around you.

- Pebbles make good paths.
- Moss and leaves can look like grass.
- Twigs make very good trees.
- Ask if you can pick flowers.

Flower heads and petals will make
it bright and colourful.

What might you use
to make a pond?
What else could you
include?

How will you make
your garden last as
long as possible?

Activity ideas

Plants are all around (pages 2-3)
- Take the children on a walk to explore their local area.
- Let the children take cameras to record what they see.
- Talk about the similarities and differences between each environment/habitat you visit.
- Make a 'local environment' display with the children.

What's in the squares? (pages 4-5)
- Talk about what might be found on a specific area of ground. How will they see the tiniest creatures? How might the children record what they see?
- Let the children measure and cut their own sticks. You may need to help them.
- Help them record what they find in whichever way they choose. Leave markers to help identify where the observation squares are.

Let's explore seeds (pages 6-7)
- Talk about what a seed is and provide examples of different types. Which can the children identify?
- Talk about the way seeds are scattered: by wind, water, explosion and animals.
- Provide fruits, vegetables and tree seeds still inside the 'fruit'. Can the children guess what the seeds will look like before you open them up?
- Help the children sort the seeds by size, colour and shape.
- Who can grow the tallest sunflower?

Get ready for planting (pages 8-9)
- Talk about the right time of year to plant different plants. Explore with the children why the timing is important.
- Make plant labels with the children to help them remember what is planted where.
- Set up a rota for watering seeds and bulbs.
- Let the children take photographs to show the growth and development of their plants. Display them with dates to encourage an understanding of time passing.

Make a composter (pages 10-11)
- Show the children examples of both compost and garden soil. What differences can they identify? Talk about the importance of nutrients for making things grow.
- Try planting seeds or bulbs both with and without compost. Which grow the best? Discuss with the children why this might be.
- Grow cress in different environments (in light/in the dark/well-watered/not well-watered). Help the children explore the needs of plants this way.

Collect and press flowers (pages 12-13)
- Talk about why petals go brown and leaves shrivel.
- Explore with the children why they should not use any flowers unless given permission.
- Collect the flowers immediately before the activity to keep them looking their best.
- Encourage the children to make pictures and individual flower pressings.

Trees (pages 14-15)
- Explore the life cycles of trees. Can they name each stage?
- Plant as many different trees as possible, both from seed, and as saplings.
- Make comparisons between trees. Compare their bark, leaves and fruit.
- Which trees can they identify by looking at the leaves?
- If you have any large trees nearby, count how many children it takes to embrace the tree.
- Introduce words such as girth, bark, foliage, coniferous and deciduous.
- Dry leaves out to make 'skeleton' leaves and ask the children to draw them.
- Make leaf and bark rubbings and discuss the similarities and differences.

Watch roots grow (pages 16-171)
- Use a camera to record how the roots develop.
- Encourage descriptive language to explain what they see happening.
- Ask the children to draw or paint what they see.

Explore pond plants (pages 18-19)
- Talk about why the leaves and flowers of some pond plants float on the surface. Encourage the children to think about weight, size and surface area. Show them that the plant's roots stretch down to the bottom of the pond. Why do they think this is necessary?
- Talk about the importance of oxygen to plants, fish, creatures and insects, and to people too.
- Make 3-D dragonflies and damselflies and hang them up to make them 'fly'.

A miniature garden (pages 20-21)
- Talk about what makes a garden e.g. grass, plants, soil.
- What do they like best in a garden and why?
- Help the children to design and make their own gardens, letting them experiment with whatever natural materials they choose.
- Provide plant mist-sprays to help them keep their gardens looking fresh.

About this book

Each book in this series provides opportunities to enhance learning and development, supporting the four main principles of the early years foundation stage: a unique child, positive relationships, enabling environments, learning and development.

Children who are given opportunities to try, to explore, to find out about their environment and to learn through both success and error will become resilient, capable, confident and self-assured. The outdoor environment is very much an enabling environment. It provides different approaches to learning in which most children thrive, with many developing greater levels of concentration and engagement in activities than they may demonstrate indoors. The freedom of the outdoors encourages positive relationships in children with both their peers and with adults, and develops independence and inner strength. All six areas of learning and development are supported across the activities in this series. Examples of these can be seen in the charts provided at www.franklinwatts.co.uk.

The activities in this book automatically lend themselves to the introduction of new language, thinking points and questioning. They encourage exploration and investigation, both as an individual, and jointly with others. Many activities can be adapted further to meet specific learning needs.

Further information

Free downloadable activity sheets
Go to www.franklinwatts.co.uk to find these free downloadable activity sheets that accompany the activities:

• A sheet to help with identification of plants in the garden (pages 2-3).
• A sheet to help with identification of plants in the pond (pages 18-19).

Forest Schools
The philosophy of Forest Schools is to encourage and inspire individuals of any age through positive outdoor experiences. Go to the website to find out what happens at a Forest School, find one local to you, learn how to set one up and more.

www.forestschools.com

IMPORTANT NOTE: An adult should supervise the activities in this book, especially those near water.

Index

First published in 2011
by Franklin Watts

Copyright © Franklin Watts 2011

Franklin Watts
338 Euston Road
London NW1 3BH

Franklin Watts Australia
Level 17/207 Kent Street
Sydney, NSW 2000

All rights reserved.

Series editor: Sarah Peutrill
Art director: Jonathan Hair
Designer: Jane Hawkins
Photography: Chris Fairclough, unless
otherwise stated

Printed in China

The Author and Publisher would like
to thank Karen Constable, reception
class teacher at Mark First School in
Somerset, for her suggestions and help
with this series. Also thanks to the
school, especially the children, for their
enthusiasm, cooperation, and sense of
fun during the photoshoots.

Dewey number: 635
ISBN: 978 1 4451 0220 7

Franklin Watts is a division of
Hachette Children's Books, an
Hachette UK company.
www.hachette.co.uk

Every attempt has been made to
clear copyright. Should there be any
inadvertent omission please apply to
the publisher for rectification.

Credits: basel101658/Shutterstock:
19t. Joerg Beuge/Shutterstock: 11tr.
Cameramannz/Shutterstock: 14c.
Jozsef Szasz-Fabian/Shutterstock:
16ca. Alex Gavaev/Shutterstock: 6t.
Tatiana Grozetskaya/Shutterstock.
16c. Joshua Haviv/Shutterstock:
3bc.Image Zebra/Shutterstock: 18t.
Yuriy Kulyk/Shutterstock: 3bl.
Marylooo/Shutterstock: 3br. Marek
Mierzeljewski/Shutterstock: 18b. Eric
Milos/Shutterstock: 14t.Picsfive/
Shutterstock: 4t. Anette Linnea
Rasmussen/Shutterstock: 6c. RT
Images/Shutterstock: 8t. Stephen
Rudolph/Shutterstock: 10b. Santje/
Shutterstock: 3cl. Edward Shaw/
istockphoto: 10c. Shebeko/Shutterstock:
16t. Anna Subbotina/Shutterstock:
2t. Swinner/Shutterstock: 3cr. Yasna/
Shutterstock: 12t.